EXPERIMENTS AND OBSERVATIONS ON ELECTRICITY MADE AT PHILADELPHIA IN AMERICA

LECTOR HOUSE PUBLIC DOMAIN WORKS

EXPERIMENTS AND OBSERVATIONS ON ELECTRICITY MADE AT PHILADELPHIA IN AMERICA

BENJAMIN FRANKLIN

ISBN: 978-93-89560-71-8

Published: 1751

LECTOR HOUSE LLP
E-MAIL: lectorpublishing@gmail.com

EXPERIMENTS AND OBSERVATIONS ON ELECTRICITY, MADE AT PHILADELPHIA IN AMERICA

AND
COMMUNICATED IN SEVERAL LETTERS
TO MR. P. COLLINSON, OF LONDON, F. R. S.

BY

MR. BENJAMIN FRANKLIN

1751

THE PREFACE.

It may be necessary to acquaint the reader, that the following observations and experiments were not drawn up with a view to their being made publick, but were communicated at different times, and most of them in letters wrote on various topicks, as matters only of private amusement.

But some persons to whom they were read, and who had themselves been conversant in electrical disquisitions, were of opinion, they contain'd so many curious and interesting particulars relative to this affair, that it would be doing a kind of injustice to the publick, to confine them solely to the limits of a private acquaintance.

The Editor was therefore prevailed upon to commit such extracts of letters, and other detach'd pieces as were in his hands to the press, without waiting for the ingenious author's permission so to do; and this was done with the less hesitation, as it was apprehended the author's engagements in other affairs, would scarce afford him leisure to give the publick his reflections and experiments on the subject, finish'd with that care and precision, of which the treatise before us shews he is alike studious and capable. He was only apprized of the step that had been thus taken, while the first sheets were in the press, and time enough for him to transmit some farther remarks, together with a few corrections and additions, which are placed at the end, and may be consulted in the perusal.

The experiments which our author relates are most of them peculiar to himself; they are conducted with judgment, and the inferences from them plain and conclusive; though sometimes proposed under the terms of suppositions and conjectures.

And indeed the scene he opens, strikes us with a pleasing astonishment, whilst he conducts us by a train of facts and judicious reflections, to a probable cause of those phænomena, which are at once the most awful, and, hitherto, accounted for with the least verisimilitude.

He exhibits to our consideration, an invisible, subtile matter, disseminated through all nature in various proportions, equally unobserved, and, whilst all those bodies to which it peculiarly adheres are alike charged with it, inoffensive.

He shews, however, that if an unequal distribution is by any means brought about; if there is a coacervation in one part of space, a less proportion, vacuity, or want, in another; by the near approach of a body capable of conducting the coacervated part to the emptier space, it becomes perhaps the most formidable and irresistible agent in the universe. Animals are in an Instant struck breathless, bodies almost impervious by any force yet known, are perforated, and metals fused by it, in a moment.

From the similar effects of lightening and electricity our author has been led to make some propable conjectures on the cause of the former; and at the same time, to propose some rational experiments in order to secure ourselves, and those things on which its force is often directed, from its pernicious effects; a circumstance of no small importance to the publick, and therefore worthy of the utmost attention.

It has, indeed, been of late the fashion to ascribe every grand or unusual operation of nature, such as lightening and earthquakes, to electricity; not, as one would imagine, from the manner of reasoning on these occasions, that the authors of these schemes have, discovered any connection betwixt the cause and effect, or saw in what manner they were related; but, as it would seem, merely because they were unacquainted with any other agent, of which it could not positively be said the connection was impossible.

But of these, and many other interesting circumstances, the reader will be more satisfactorily informed in the following letters, to which he is therefore referred by

The EDITOR.

CONTENTS

LETTER I.

FROM
MR BENJ. FRANKLIN, IN PHILADELPHIA.
TO
MR PETER COLLINSON, F.R.S. LONDON.

July 28, 1747.

SIR,

THE necessary trouble of copying long letters, which perhaps when they come to your hands may contain nothing new, or worth your reading (so quick is the progress made with you in Electricity) half discourages me from writing any more on that subject. Yet I cannot forbear adding a few observations on M. *Muschenbroek*'s wonderful bottle.

1. The non-electric contain'd in the bottle differs when electrised from a non-electric electrised out of the bottle, in this: that the electrical fire of the latter is accumulated *on its surface*, and forms an electrical atmosphere round it of considerable extent: but the electrical fire is crouded *into the substance* of the former, the glass confining it.

2. At the same time that the wire and top of the bottle, &c. is electrised *positively* or *plus*, the bottom of the bottle is electrised *negatively* or *minus*, in exact proportion: *i. e.* whatever quantity of electrical fire is thrown in at top, an equal quantity goes out of the bottom. To understand this, suppose the common quantity of Electricity in each part of the bottle, before the operation begins, is equal to 20; and at every stroke of the tube, suppose a quantity equal to 1 is thrown in; then, after the first stroke, the quantity contain'd in the wire and upper part of the bottle will be 21, in the bottom 19. After the second, the upper part will have 22, the lower 18, and so on 'till after 20 strokes, the upper part will have a quantity of electrical fire equal to 40, the lower part none: and then the operation ends: for no more can be thrown into the upper part, when no more can be driven out of the lower part. If you attempt to throw more in, it is spued back thro' the wire, or flies out in loud cracks thro' the sides of the bottle.

3. The equilibrium cannot be restored in the bottle by *inward* communication or contact of the parts; but it must be done by a communication formed *without* the bottle, between the top and bottom, by some non-electric, touching both at the same time; in which case it is restored with a violence and quickness inexpressible: or, touching each alternately, in which case the equilibrium is restored by degrees.

4. As no more electrical fire can be thrown into the top of the bottle, when all is driven out of the bottom, so in a bottle not yet electrised, none can be thrown into the top, when none *can* get out at the bottom; which happens either when the bottom is too thick, or when the bottle is placed on an electric *per se*. Again, when the bottle is electrised, but little of the electrical fire can be *drawn out* from the top, by touching the wire, unless an equal quantity can at the same time *get in* at the bottom. Thus, place an electrised bottle on clean glass or dry wax, and you will not, by touching the wire, get out the fire from the top. Place it on a non-electric, and touch the wire, you will get it out in a short time; but soonest when you form a direct communication as above.

So wonderfully are these two states of Electricity, the *plus* and *minus*, combined and balanced in this miraculous bottle! situated and related to each other in a manner that I can by no means comprehend! If it were possible that a bottle should in one part contain a quantity of air strongly comprest, and in another part a perfect vacuum, we know the equilibrium would be instantly restored *within*. But here we have a bottle containing at the same time a *plenum* of electrical fire, and a *vacuum* of the same fire; and yet the equilibrium cannot be restored between them but by a communication *without*! though the *plenum* presses violently to expand, and the hungry vacuum seems to attract as violently in order to be filled.

5. The shock to the nerves (or convulsion rather) is occasion'd by the sudden passing of the fire through the body in its way from the top to the bottom of the bottle. The fire takes the shortest course, as Mr *Watson* justly observes: But it does not appear, from experiment, that, in order for a person to be shocked, a communication with the floor is necessary; for he that holds the bottle with one hand, and touches the wire with the other, will be shock'd as much, though his shoes be dry, or even standing on wax, as otherwise. And on the touch of the wire (or of the gun-barrel, which is the same thing) the fire does not proceed from the touching finger to the wire, as is supposed, but from the wire to the finger, and passes through the body to the other hand, and so into the bottom of the bottle.

EXPERIMENTS *confirming the above.*

EXPERIMENT I.

Place an electrised phial on wax; a small cork-ball suspended by a dry silk-thread held in your hand, and brought near to the wire, will first be attracted, and then repelled: when in this state of repellency, sink your hand, that the ball may be brought towards the bottom of the bottle; it will there be instantly and strongly attracted, 'till it has parted with its fire.

If the bottle had an electrical atmosphere, as well as the wire, an electrified cork would be repelled from one as well as from the cther.

EXPERIMENT II.

FIG. 1. From a bent wire (*a*) sticking in the table, let a small linen thread (*b*) hang down within half an inch of the electrised phial (*c*). Touch the wire of the phial repeatedly with your finger, and at every touch you will see the thread instantly attracted by the bottle. (This is best done by a vinegar cruet, or some such belly'd bottle). As soon as you draw any fire out from the upper part by touching the wire, the lower part of the bottle draws an equal quantity ir. by the thread.

EXPERIMENT III.

FIG. 2. Fix a wire in the lead, with which the bottom of the bottle is armed, (*d*) so as that bending upwards, its ring-end may be level with the top or ring-end of the wire in the cork (*e*), and at three or four inches distance. Then electricise the bottle, and place it on wax. If a cork suspended by a silk thread (*f*) hang between these two wires, it will play incessantly from one to the other, 'till the bottle is no longer electrised; that is, it fetches and carries fire from the top to the bottom of the bottle, 'till the equilibrium is restored.

EXPERIMENT IV.

FIG. 3. Place an electricised phial on wax; take a wire (*g*) in form of a C, the ends at such a distance when bent, as that the upper may touch the wire of the bottle, when the lower touches the bottom: stick the outer part on a stick of sealing wax (*h*) which will serve as a handle. Then apply the lower end to the bottom of the bottle, and gradually bring the upper-end near the wire in the cork. The consequence is, spark follows spark till the equilibrium is restored. Touch the top first, and on approaching the bottom with the other end, you have a constant stream of fire, from the wire entering the bottle. Touch the tcp and bottom together, and the equilibrium will soon be restored, but silently and imperceptibly; the crooked wire forming the communication.

EXPERIMENT V.

FIG. 4. Let a ring of thin lead or paper surround a bottle (*i*), even at some distance from or above the bottom. From that ring let a wire proceed up, 'till it touch the wire of the cork (*k*). A bottle so fixt cannot by any means be electrised: the equilibrium is never destroyed: for while the communication between the upper and lower parts of the bottle is continued by the outside wire, the fire only circulates: what is driven out at bottom, is constantly supply'd from the top. Hence a bottle cannot be electrised that is foul or moist on the outside.

EXPERIMENT VI.

Place a man on a cake of wax, and present him the wire of the electrified phial to touch, you standing on the floor, and holding it in your hand. As often as he touches it, he will be electrified *plus*; and any one standing on the floor may draw a spark from him. The fire in this experiment passes cut of the wire into him; and at the same time out of your hand into the bottom of the bottle.

EXPERIMENT VII.

Give him the electrified phial to hold; and do you touch the wire; as often you touch it he will be electrified *minus*, and may draw a spark from any one standing on the floor. The fire now passes from the wire to you, and from him into the bottom of the bottle.

EXPERIMENT VIII.

Lay two books on two glasses, back towards back, two or three Inches distant. Set the electrified phial on one, and then touch the wire; that book will be electrified *minus*; the electrical fire being drawn out of it by the bottom of the bottle. Take off the bottle, and holding it in your hand, touch the other with the wire; that book will be electrised *plus*; the fire passing into it from the wire, and the bottle at the same time supply'd from your hand. A suspended small cork-ball will play between these books 'till the equilibrium is restored.

EXPERIMENT IX.

When a body is electrised *plus* it will repel an electrified feather or small cork-ball. When *minus* (or when in the common state) it will attract them, but stronger when *minus* than when in the common state, the difference being greater.

EXPERIMENT X.

Tho', as in EXPER. VI. a man standing on wax may be electrised a number of times, by repeatedly touching the wire of an electrised bottle (held in the hand of one standing on the floor) he receiving the fire from the wire each time: yet holding it in his own hand, and touching the wire, tho' he draws a strong spark, and is violently shock'd, no Electricity remains in him; the fire only passing thro' him from the upper to the lower part of the bottle. Observe, before the shock, to let some one on the floor touch him to restore the equilibrium in his body; for in taking hold of the bottom of the bottle, he sometimes becomes a little electrised *minus*, which will continue after the shock; as would also any *plus* Electricity, which he might have given him before the shock. For, restoring the equilibrium in the bottle does not at all affect the Electricity in the man thro' whom the fire passes; that Electricity is neither increased nor diminish'd.

EXPERIMENT XI.

The passing of the electrical fire from the upper to the lower part of the bottle, to restore the equilibrium is render'd strongly visible by the following pretty experiment. Take a book whose cover is filletted with gold; bend a wire of eight or ten inches long in the form of (*m*) Fig. 5, slip it on the end of the cover of the book over the gold line, so as that the shoulder of it may press upon one end of the gold line, the ring up, but leaning towards the other end of the book. Lay the book on a glass or wax; and on the other end of the gold lines, set the bottle electrised: then bend the springing wire, by pressing it with a stick of wax till its ring approaches the ring of the bottle wire; instantly there is a strong spark and stroke, and the whole line of gold, which completes the communication between the top and bottom of the bottle, will appear a vivid flame, like the sharpest lightning. The closer the contact between the shoulder of the wire, and the gold at one end of the line, and between the bottom of the bottle and the gold at the other end, the better the experiment succeeds. The room should be darkened. If you would have the whole filletting round the cover appear in fire at once, let the bottle and wire touch the gold in the diagonally opposite corners.

I am, &c.
B. FRANKLIN.

LETTER II.

FROM
MR BENJ. FRANKLIN, IN PHILADELPHIA.
TO
MR PETER COLLINSON, F.R.S. LONDON.

Sept. 1, 1747.

SIR,

In my last I informed you that, in pursuing our electrical enquiries, we had observed some particular Phænomena, which we looked upon to be new, and of which I promised to give you some account, tho' I apprehended they might possibly not be new to you, as so many hands are daily employ'd in electrical experiments on your side the water, some or other of which would probably hit on the same observations.

The first is the wonderful effect of pointed bodies, both in *drawing off* and *throwing off* the electrical fire. For example:

Place an iron shot of three or four inches diameter, on the mouth of a clean dry glass bottle. By a fine silken thread from the cieling, right over the mouth of the bottle, suspend a small cork-ball, about the bigness of a marble; the thread of such a length, as that the cork-ball may rest against the side of the shot. Electrify the shot, and the ball will be repelled to the distance of four or five inches, more or less, according to the quantity of Electricity.—When in this state, if you present to the shot the point of a long slender sharp bodkin, at six or eight inches distance, the repellency is instantly destroy'd, and the cork flies to the shot. A blunt body must be brought within an inch, and draw a spark, to produce the same effect. To prove that the electrical fire is *drawn off* by the point, if you take the blade of the bodkin out of the wooden handle, and fix it in a stick of sealing wax, and then present it at the distance aforesaid, or if you bring it very near, no such effect follows; but sliding one finger along the wax till you touch the blade, and the ball flies to the shot immediately.—If you present the point in the dark, you will see, sometimes at a foot distance, and more, a light gather upon it like that of a fire-fly or glow-worm; the less sharp the point, the nearer you must bring it to observe the light; and at whatever distance you see the light, you may draw off the electrical fire, and destroy the repellency.—If a cork-ball so suspended be repelled by the tube, and a point be presented quick to it, tho' at a considerable distance, 'tis surprizing to see how suddenly it flies back to the tube. Points of wood will do as well as those of iron, provided the wood is not dry; for perfectly dry wood will no more conduct Electricity than sealing wax.

To shew that points will *throw off* as well as *draw off* the electrical fire; lay a long sharp needle upon the shot, and you cannot electrise the shot, so as to make it repel the cork-ball.—Or fix a needle to the end of a suspended gun-barrel, or iron rod, so as to point beyond it like a little bayonet; and while it remains there, the gun-barrel, or rod, cannot by applying the tube to the other end be electrised so as to give a spark, the fire continually running out silently at the point. In the dark you may see it make the same appearance as it does in the case beforementioned.

The repellency between the cork-ball and the shot is likewise destroy'd; 1. By sifting fine sand on it; this does it gradually. 2. By breathing on it. 3. By making a smoke about it from burning wood.[1] 4. By candle light, even tho' the candle is at a foot distance: these do it suddenly.—The light of a bright coal from a wood fire; and the light of red-hot iron do it likewise; but not at so great a distance. Smoke from dry rosin dropt on hot iron, does not destroy the repellency; but is attracted by both shot and cork-ball, forming proportionable atmospheres round them, making them look beautifully, somewhat like some of the figures in *Burnet*'s or *Whiston*'s theory of the earth.

N. B. This experiment should be made in a closet where the air is very still.

The light of the sun thrown strongly on both cork and shot by a looking-glass for a long time together, does not impair the repellency in the least. This difference between fire-light and sun-light, is another thing that seems new and extraordinary to us.

We had for some time been of opinion, that the electrical fire was not created by friction, but collected, being really an element diffus'd among, and attracted by other matter, particularly by water and metals. We had even discovered and demonstrated its afflux to the electrical sphere, as well as its efflux, by means of little light windmill wheels made of stiff paper vanes, fixed obliquely and turning freely on fine wire axes. Also by little wheels of the same matter, but formed like water wheels. Of the disposition and application of which wheels, and the various phænomena resulting, I could, if I had time, fill you a sheet. The impossibility of electrising one's self (tho' standing on wax) by rubbing the tube and drawing the fire from it; and the manner of doing it by passing the tube near a person or thing standing on the floor, &c. had also occurred to us some months before Mr *Watson*'s ingenious *Sequel* came to hand, and these were some of the new things I intended to have communicated to you.—But now I need only mention some particulars not hinted in that piece, with our reasonings thereupon; though perhaps the latter might well enough be spared.

---

[1] We suppose every particle of sand, moisture, or smoke, being first attracted and then repelled, carries off with it a portion of the electrical fire; but that the same still subsists in those particles, till they communicate it to something else; and that it is never really destroyed.—So when water is thrown on common fire, we do not imagine the element is thereby destroyed or annihilated, but only dispersed, each particle of water carrying off in vapour its portion of the fire, which it had attracted and attached to itself.

1. A person standing on wax, and rubbing the tube, and another person on wax drawing the fire; they will both of them, (provided they do not stand so as to touch one another) appear to be electrised, to a person standing on the floor; that is, he will perceive a spark on approaching each of them with his knuckle.

2. But if the persons on wax touch one another during the exciting of the tube, neither of them will appear to be electrised.

3. If they touch one another after exciting the tube, and drawing the fire as aforesaid, there will be a stronger spark between them, than was between either of them and the person on the floor.

4. After such strong spark, neither of them discover any electricity.

These appearances we attempt to account for thus. We suppose as aforesaid, that electrical fire is a common element, of which every one of the three persons abovementioned has his equal share, before any operation is begun with the Tube. *A*, who stands on wax and rubs the tube collects the electrical fire from himself into the glass; and his communication with the common stock being cut off by the wax, his body is not again immediately supply'd. *B*, (who stands on wax likewise) passing his knuckle along near the tube, receives the fire which was collected by the glass from *A*; and his communication with the common stock being likewise cut off, he retains the additional quantity received.—To *C*, standing on the floor, both appear to be electrised: for he having only the middle quantity of electrical fire, receives a spark upon approaching *B*, who has an over quantity; but gives one to *A*, who has an under quantity. If *A* and *B* approach to touch each other, the spark is stronger, because the difference between them is greater; after such touch there is no spark between either of them and *C*, because the electrical fire in all is reduced to the original equality. If they touch while electrising, the equality is never destroy'd, the fire only circulating. Hence have arisen some new terms among us: we say, *B*, (and bodies like circumstanced) is electrised *positively*; *A*, *negatively*. Or rather, *B* is electrised *plus*; *A*, *minus*. And we daily in our experiments electrise bodies *plus* or *minus* as we think proper.—To electrise *plus* or *minus*, no more needs to be known than this, that the parts of the tube or sphere that are rubbed, do, in the instant of the friction attract the electrical fire, and therefore take it from the thing rubbing: the same parts immediately, as the friction upon them ceases, are disposed to give the fire they have received, to any body that has less. Thus you may circulate it, as Mr *Watson* has shewn; you may also accumulate or substract it upon or from any body, as you connect that body with the rubber or with the receiver, the communication with the common stock being cut off. We think that ingenious gentleman was deceived, when he imagined (in his *Sequel*) that the electrical fire came down the wire from the cieling to the gun-barrel, thence to the sphere, and so electrised the machine and the man turning the wheel, *&c.* We suppose it was *driven off*, and not brought on thro' that wire; and that the machine and man, *&c.* were electrised *minus*; *i. e.* had less electrical fire in them than things in common.

As the vessel is just upon sailing, I cannot give you so large an account of American Electricity as I intended: I shall only mention a few particulars more.—

We find granulated lead better to fill the phial with, than water, being easily warmed, and keeping warm and dry in damp air. — We fire spirits with the wire of the phial. — We light candles, just blown out, by drawing a spark among the smoke between the wire and snuffers. — We represent lightning, by passing the wire in the dark over a china plate that has gilt flowers, or applying it to gilt frames of looking-glasses, &c. — We electrise a person twenty or more times running, with a touch of the finger on the wire, thus: He stands on wax. Give him the electrised bottle in his hand. Touch the wire with your finger, and then touch his hand or face; there are sparks every time. — We encrease the force of the electrical kiss vastly, thus: Let *A* and *B* stand on wax; give one of them the electrised phial in hand; let the other take hold of the wire; there will be a small spark; but when their lips approach, they will be struck and shock'd. The same if another gentleman and lady, *C* and *D*, standing also on wax, and joining hands with *A* and *B*, salute, or shake hands. — We suspend by fine silk thread a counterfeit spider, made of a small piece of burnt cork, with legs of linnen thread, and a grain or two of lead stuck in him to give him more weight. Upon the table, over which he hangs, we stick a wire upright as high as the phial and wire, two or three inches from the spider; then we animate him by setting the electrified phial at the same distance on the other side of him; he will immediately fly to the wire of the phial, bend his legs in touching it, then spring off, and fly to the wire in the table; thence again to the wire of the phial, playing with his legs against both in a very entertaining manner, appearing perfectly alive to persons unacquainted. He will continue this motion an hour or more in dry weather. — We electrify, upon wax in the dark, a book that has a double line of gold round upon the covers, and then apply a knuckle to the gilding; the fire appears every where upon the gold like a flash of lightning: not upon the leather, nor, if you touch the leather instead of the gold. We rub our tubes with buckskin, and observe always to keep the same side to the tube, and never to sully the tube by handling; thus they work readily and easily, without the least fatigue; especially if kept in tight pastboard cases, lined with flannel, and fitting closeto the tube.[2] — This I mention because the *European* papers, on Electricity, frequently speak of rubbing the tube, as a fatiguing exercise. Our spheres are fixed on iron axes, which pass through them. At one end of the axis there is a small handle, with which we turn the sphere like a common grindstone. This we find very commodious, as the machine takes up but little room, is portable, and may be enclosed in a tight box, when not in use. 'Tis true, the sphere does not turn so swift, as when the great wheel is used: but swiftness we think of little importance, since a few turns will charge the phial, &c. sufficiently.

I am, &c.
B. FRANKLIN.

---

[2] Our tubes are made here of green glass, 27 or 30 inches long, as big as can be grasped. Electricity is so much in vogue, that above one hundred of them have been sold within these four months past.

LETTER III.

FROM
MR BENJ. FRANKLIN, IN PHILADELPHIA.
TO
MR PETER COLLINSON, F.R.S. LONDON.

Farther EXPERIMENTS *and* OBSERVATIONS *in* ELECTRICITY.

1748.

SIR,

§ 1. There will be the same explosion and shock, if the electrified phial is held in one hand by the hook, and the coating touch›d with the other, as when held by the coating, and touch›d at the hook.

2. To take the charg'd phial safely by the hook, and not at the same time diminish its force, it must first be set down on an electric *per se.*

3. The phial will be electrified as strongly, if held by the hook, and the coating apply'd to the globe or tube; as when held by the coating, and the hook apply'd.

4. But the *direction* of the electrical fire being different in the charging, will also be different in the explosion. The bottle charged thro' the hook, will be discharged thro' the hook; the bottle charged thro' the coating, will be discharged thro' the coating, and not other ways: for the fire must come out the same way it went in.

5. To prove this; take two bottles that were equally charged thro' the hooks, one in each hand; bring their hooks near each other, and no spark or shock will follow; because each hook is disposed to give fire, and neither to receive it. Set one of the bottles down on glass, take it up by the hook, and apply its coating to the hook of the other; then there will be an explosion and shock, and both bottles will be discharged.

6. Vary the experiment, by charging two phials equally, one thro' the hook, the other thro' the coating: hold that by the coating which was charged thro' the hook; and that by the hook which was charg'd thro' the coating: apply the hook of the first to the coating of the other, and there will be no shock or spark. Set that down on glass which you held by the hook, take it up by the coating, and bring the two hooks together: a spark and shock will follow, and both phials be discharged.

In this experiment the bottles are totally discharged, or the equilibrium within them restored. The *abounding* of fire in one of the hooks (or rather in the internal surface of one bottle) being exactly equal to the *wanting* of the other: and therefore, as each bottle has in itself the *abounding* as well as the *wanting*, the wanting and abounding must be equal in each bottle. See §. 8, 9, 10, 11. But if a man holds in his hands two bottles, one fully electrify'd, the other not at all, and brings their hooks together, he has but half a shock, and the bottles will both remain half electrified, the one being half discharged, and the other half charged.

7. Place two phials equally charged on a table at five or six inches distance. Let a cork-ball, suspended by a silk thread, hang between them. If the phials were both charged through their hooks, the cork, when it has been attracted and repell'd by the one, will not be attracted, but equally repelled by the other. But if the phials were charged, the one through the hook, and the other[3] through the coating, the ball, when it is repelled from one hook, will be as strongly attracted by the other, and play vigorously between them, 'till both phials are nearly discharged.

8. When we use the terms of *charging* and *discharging* the phial, 'tis in compliance with custom, and for want of others more suitable. Since we are of opinion, that there is really no more electrical fire in the phial after what is called its *charging*, than before, nor less after its *discharging*; excepting only the small spark that might be given to, and taken from, the non-electric matter, if separated from the bottle, which spark may not be equal to a five hundredth part of what is called the explosion.

For if, on the explosion, the electrical fire came out of the bottle by one part, and did not enter in again by another; then, if a man standing on wax, and holding the bottle in one hand, takes the spark by touching the wire hook with the other, the bottle being thereby *discharged*, the man would be *charged*; or whatever fire was lost by one, would be found in the other, since there is no way for its escape: But the contrary is true.

9. Besides the phial will not suffer what is called a *charging*, unless as much fire can go out of it one way, as is thrown in by another. A phial cannot be charged standing on wax or glass, or hanging on the prime conductor, unless a communication be form'd between its coating and the floor.

10. But suspend two or more phials on the prime conductor, one hanging to the tail of the other; and a wire from the last to the floor, an equal number of turns of the wheel shall charge them all equally, and every one as much as one alone would have been. What is driven out at the tail of the first, serving to charge the second; what is driven out of the second charging the third; and so on. By this means a great number of bottles might be charged with the same labour, and equally high, with one alone, were it not that every bottle receives new fire, and loses its old with some reluctance, or rather gives some small resistance to the charging, which in a number of bottles becomes more equal to the charging power, and so repels the fire back again on the globe, sooner than a single bottle would do.

---

[3] To charge a bottle commodiously through the coating, place it on a glass stand; form a communication from the prime conductor to the coating, and another from the hook to the wall or floor. When it is charged, remove the latter communication before you take hold of the bottle, otherwise great part of the fire will escape by it.

11. When a bottle is charged in the common way, its *inside* and *outside* surfaces stand ready, the one to give fire by the hook, the other to receive it by the coating; the one is full, and ready to throw out, the other empty and extremely hungry; yet as the first will not *give out*, unless the other can at the same instant *receive in*; so neither will the latter receive in, unless the first can at the same instant give out. When both can be done at once, 'tis done with inconceivable quickness and violence.

12. So a strait spring (tho' the comparison does not agree in every particular) when forcibly bent, must, to restore itself, contract that side which in the bending was extended, and extend that which was contracted: if either of these two operations be hindered, the other cannot be done. But the spring is not said to be *charg'd* with elasticity when bent, and discharg'd when unbent; its quantity of elasticity is always the same.

13. Glass, in like manner, has, within its substance, always the same quantity of electrical fire, and that a very great quantity in proportion to the mass of glass, as shall be shewn hereafter.

14. This quantity, proportioned to the glass, it strongly and obstinately retains, and will have neither more nor less, though it will suffer a change to be made in its parts and situation; *i. e.* we may take away part of it from one of the sides, provided we throw an equal quantity into the other.

15. Yet when the situation of the electrical fire is thus altered in the glass; when some has been taken from one side, and some added to the other, it will not be at rest or in its natural state, till 'tis restored to its original equality.—And this restitution cannot be made through the substance of the glass, but must be done by a non-electric communication formed without, from surface to surface.

16. Thus, the whole force of the bottle, and power of giving a shock, is in the GLASS ITSELF; the non-electrics in contact with the two surfaces, serving only to *give* and *receive* to and from the several parts of the glass; that is, to give on one side, and take away from the other.

17. This was discovered here in the following manner. Purposing to analyse the electrified bottle, in order to find wherein its strength lay, we placed it on glass, and drew out the cork and wire which for that purpose had been loosely put in. Then taking the bottle in one hand, and bringing a finger of the other near its mouth, a strong spark came from the water, and the shock was as violent as if the wire had remained in it, which shewed that the force did not lie in the wire. Then to find if it resided in the water, being crouded into and condensed in it, as connfi'd by the glass, which had been our former opinion, we electrify'd the bottle again, and placing it on glass, drew out the wire and cork as before; then taking up the bottle we decanted all its water into an empty bottle, which likewise stood on glass; and taking up that other bottle, we expected if the force resided in the water, to find a shock from it; but there was none. We judged then, that it must either be lost in decanting, or remain in the first bottle. The latter we found to be true: for that bottle on trial gave the shock, though filled up as it stood with fresh unelectrified water from a tea-pot.—To find then, whether glass had this property

merely as glass, or whether the form contributed any thing to it; we took a pane of sash-glass, and laying it on the stand, placed a plate of lead on its upper surface; then electrify'd that plate, and bringing a finger to it, there was a spark and shock. We then took two plates of lead of equal dimensions, but less than the glass by two inches every way, and electrified the glass between them, by electrifying the uppermost lead; then separated the glass from the lead, in doing which, what little fire might be in the lead was taken out and the glass being touched in the electrified parts with a finger, afforded only very small pricking sparks, but a great number of them might be taken from different places. Then dexterously placing it again between the leaden plates, and compleating a circle between the two surfaces, a violent shock ensued.—Which demonstrated the power to reside in glass as glass, and that the non-electrics in contact served only, like the armature of a loadstone, to unite the force of the several parts, and bring them at once to any point desired: it being a property of a non-electric, that the whole body instantly receives or gives what electrical fire is given to or taken from any one of its parts.

18. Upon this, we made what we call'd an *electrical-battery*, consisting of eleven panes of large sash-glass, arm'd with thin leaden plates pasted on each side, placed vertically, and supported at two inches distance on silk cords, with thick hooks of leaden wire, one from each side, standing upright, distant from each other, and convenient communications of wire and chain, from the giving side of one pane, to the receiving side of the other; that so the whole might be charged together, and with the same labour as one single pane; and another contrivance to bring the giving sides, after charging, in contact with one long wire, and the receivers with another, which two long wires would give the force of all the plates of glass at once through the body of any animal forming the circle with them. The plates may also be discharged separately, or any number together that is required. But this machine is not much used, as not perfectly answering our intention with regard to the ease of charging, for the reason given § 10. We made also of large glass panes, magical pictures, and self-moving animated wheels, presently to be described.

19. I perceive by the ingenious Mr *Watson*'s last book, lately received, that Dr *Bevis* had used, before we had, panes of glass to give a shock; though, till that book came to hand, I thought to have communicated it to you as a novelty. The excuse for mentioning it here, is, that we tried the experiment differently, drew different consequences from it, (for Mr *Watson* still seems to think the fire *accumulated on the non-electric* that is in contact with the glass, page 72) and, as far as we hitherto know, have carried it farther.

20. The magical picture is made thus. Having a large metzotinto with a frame and glass, suppose of the KING, (God preserve him) take out the print, and cut a pannel out of it, near two inches distant from the frame all round. If the cut is through the picture 'tis not the worse. With thin paste or gum-water, fix the border that is cut off on the inside of the glass, pressing it smooth and close; then fill up the vacancy by gilding the glass well with leaf gold or brass. Gild likewise the inner edge of the back of the frame all round except the top part, and form a communication between that gilding and the gilding behind the glass: then put in the board, and that side is finished. Turn up the glass, and gild the fore side exactly

over the back gilding, and when it is dry, cover it by pasting on the pannel of the picture that had been cut out, observing to bring the corresponding parts of the border and picture together, by which the picture will appear of a piece as at first, only part is behind the glass, and part before.—Hold the picture horizontally by the top, and place a little moveable gilt crown on the king's-head. If now the picture be moderately electrified, and another person take hold of the frame with one hand, so that his fingers touch its inside gilding, and with the other hand endeavour to take off the crown, he will receive a terrible blow, and fail in the attempt. If the picture were highly charged, the consequence might perhaps be as fatal as that of high-treason; for when the spark is taken through a quire of paper laid on the picture, by means of a wire communication, it makes a fair hole through every sheet, that is, through 48 leaves, (though a quire of paper is thought good armour against the push of a sword or even against a pistol bullet) and the crack is exceeding loud. The operator, who holds the picture by the upper-end, where the inside of the frame is not gilt, to prevent its falling, feels nothing of the shock, and may touch the face of the picture without danger, which he pretends is a test of his loyalty.—If a ring of persons take the shock among them, the experiment is called, *The Conspirators.*

21. On the principle, in § 7, that hooks of bottles, differently charged, will attract and repel differently, is made, an electrical wheel, that turns with considerable strength. A small upright shaft of wood passes at right angles through a thin round board, of about twelve inches diameter, and turns on a sharp point of iron fixed in the lower end, while a strong wire in the upper-end passing thro' a small hole in a thin brass plate, keeps the shaft truly vertical. About thirty *radii* of equal length, made of sash glass cut in narrow strips, issue horizontally from the circumference of the board, the ends most distant from the center being about four inches apart. On the end of every one, a brass thimble is fixed. If now the wire of a bottle electrified in the common way, be brought near the circumference of this wheel, it will attract the nearest thimble, and so put the wheel in motion; that thimble, in passing by, receives a spark, and thereby being electrified is repelled and so driven forwards; while a second being attracted, approaches the wire, receives a spark, and is driven after the first, and so on till the wheel has gone once round, when the thimbles before electrified approaching the wire, instead of being attracted as they were at first, are repelled, and the motion presently ceases.—But if another bottle which had been charged through the coating be placed near the same wheel, its wire will attract the thimble repelled by the first, and thereby double the force that carries the wheel round; and not only taking out the fire that had been communicated to the thimbles by the first bottle, but even robbing them of their natural quantity, instead of being repelled when they come again towards the first bottle, they are more strongly attracted, so that the wheel mends its pace, till it goes with great rapidity twelve or fifteen rounds in a minute, and with such strength, as that the weight of one hundred *Spanish* dollars with which we once loaded it, did not seem in the least to retard its motion.—This is called an electrical jack; and if a large fowl were spitted on the upright shaft, it would be carried round before a fire with a motion fit for roasting.

22. But this wheel, like those driven by wind, water, or weights, moves by a foreign force, to wit, that of the bottles. The self-moving wheel, though constructed on the same principles, appears more surprising. 'Tis made of a thin round plate of window-glass, seventeen inches diameter, well gilt on both sides, all but two inches next the edge. Two small hemispheres of wood are then fixed with cement to the middle of the upper and under sides, centrally opposite, and in each of them a thick strong wire eight or ten inches long, which together make the axis of the wheel. It turns horizontally on a point at the lower end of its Axis, which rests on a bit of brass cemented within a glass salt-celler. The upper end of its axis passes thro' a hole in a thin brass plate cemented to a long strong piece of glass, which keeps it six or eight inches distant from any non-electric, and has a small ball of wax or metal on its top to keep in the fire. In a circle on the table which supports the wheel, are fixed twelve small pillars of glass, at about four inches distance, with a thimble on the top of each. On the edge of the wheel is a small leaden bullet communicating by a wire with the gilding of the *upper* surface of the wheel; and about six inches from it is another bullet communicating in like manner with the *under* surface. When the wheel is to be charged by the upper surface, a communication must be made from the under surface to the table. When it is well charg'd it begins to move; the bullet nearest to a pillar moves towards the thimble on that pillar, and passing by electrifies it and then pushes itself from it; the succeeding bullet, which communicates with the other surface of the glass, more strongly attracts that thimble on account of its being before electrified by the other bullet; and thus the wheel encreases its motion till it comes to such a height as that the resistance of the air regulates it. It will go half an hour, and make one minute with another twenty turns in a minute, which is six hundred turns in the whole; the bullet of the upper surface giving in each turn twelve sparks, to the thimbles, which make seven thousand two hundred sparks; and the bullet of the under surface receiving as many from the thimbles; those bullets moving in the time near two thousand five hundred feet.—The thimbles are well fixed, and in so exact a circle, that the bullets may pass within a very small distance of each of them.—If instead of two bullets you put eight, four communicating with the upper surface, and four with the under surface, placed alternately; which eight, at about six inches distance, compleats the circumference, the force and swiftness will be greatly increased, the wheel making fifty turns in a minute; but then it will not continue moving so long.—These wheels may be applied, perhaps, to the ringing of chimes, and moving of light-made Orreries.

23. A small wire bent circularly with a loop at each end; let one end rest against the under surface of the wheel, and bring the other end near the upper surface, it will give a terrible crack, and the force will be discharged.

24. Every spark in that manner drawn from the surface of the wheel, makes a round hole in the gilding, tearing off a part of it in coming out; which shews that the fire is not accumulated on the gilding, but is in the glass itself.

25. The gilding being varnish'd over with turpentine varnish, the varnish tho' dry and hard, is burnt by the spark drawn thro' it, and gives a strong smell and visible smoke. And when the spark is drawn through paper, all round the hole

made by it, the paper will be blacked by the smoke, which sometimes penetrates several of the leaves. Part of the gilding torn off, is also found forcibly driven into the hole made in the paper by the stroke.

26. 'Tis amazing to observe in how small a portion of glass a great electrical force may lie. A thin glass bubble, about an inch diameter, weighing only six grains, being half-filled with water, partly gilt on the outside, and furnish'd with a wire hook, gives, when electrified, as great a shock as a man can well bear. As the glass is thickest near the orifice, I suppose the lower half, which being gilt was electrified, and gave the shock, did not exceed two grains; for it appeared, when broke, much thinner than the upper half. — If one of these thin bottles be electrified by the coating, and the spark taken out thro' the gilding, it will break the glass inwards at the same time that it breaks the gilding outwards.

27. And allowing (for the reasons before given, § 8, 9, 10,) that there is no more electrical fire in a bottle after charging, than before, how great must be the quantity in this small portion of glass! It seems as if it were of its very substance and essence. Perhaps if that due quantity of electrical fire so obstinately retained by glass, could be separated from it, it would no longer be glass; it might lose its transparency, or its brittleness, or its elasticity. — Experiments may possibly be invented hereafter, to discover this.

27. We are surprized at the account given in Mr *Watson*'s book, of a shock communicated through a great space of dry ground, and suspect there must be some metaline quality in the gravel of that ground; having found that simple dry earth, rammed in a glass tube, open at both ends, and a wire hook inserted in the earth at each end, the earth and wires making part of a circle, would not conduct the least perceptible shock, and indeed when one wire was electrify'd, the other hardly showed any signs of its being in connection with it. — Even a thoroughly wet pack-thread sometimes fails of conducting a shock, tho' it otherwise conducts electricity very well. A dry cake of ice, or an icicle held between two in a circle, likewise prevents the shock; which one would not expect, as water conducts it so perfectly well. — Gilding on a new book, though at first it conducts the shock extremely well, yet fails after ten or a dozen experiments, though it appears otherwise in all respects the same, which we cannot account for.

28. There is one experiment more which surprizes us, and is not hitherto satisfactorily accounted for; it is this. Place an iron shot on a glass stand, and let a ball of damp cork, suspended by a silk thread, hang in contact with the shot. Take a bottle in each hand, one that is electrify'd through the hook, the other through the coating: Apply the giving wire to the shot, which will electrify it *positively*, and the cork shall be repelled: Then apply the requiring wire, which will take out the spark given by the other; when the cork will return to the shot: Apply the same again, and take out another spark, so will the shot be electrify'd *negatively*; and the cork in that case shall be repelled equally as before. Then apply the giving wire to the shot, and give the spark it wanted, so will the cork return: Give it another, which will be an addition to its natural quantity, so will the cork be repelled again: And so may the experiment be repeated as long as there is any charge in the bottles. Which shews that bodies having less than the common quantity of Electricity, repel each

other, as well as those that have more.

Chagrined a little that we have hitherto been able to produce nothing in this way of use to mankind; and the hot weather coming on, when electrical experiments are not so agreeable, 'tis proposed to put an end to them for this season, somewhat humorously, in a party of pleasure, on the banks of *Skuylkill*.[4] Spirits, at the same time, are to be fired by a spark sent from side to side through the river, without any other conductor than the water; an experiment which we some time since performed, to the amazement of many. A turkey is to be killed for our dinner by the *electrical shock*, and roasted by the *electrical jack*, before a fire kindled by the *electrified bottle*; when the healths of all the famous electricians in *England*, *Holland*, *France*, and *Germany*, are to be drank in[5]*electrified bumpers*, under the discharge of guns from the *electrical battery*.

April 29, 1749.

---

[4] The river that washes one side of *Philadelphia*, as the *Delaware* does the other; both are ornamented with the summer habitations, of the citizens, and the agreeable mansions of the principal people of this colony.

[5] An electrified bumper, is a small thin glass tumbler, near filled with wine, and electrified as the bottle. This when brought to the lips gives a shock, if the party be close shaved, and does not breathe on the liquor.

LETTER IV.

CONTAINING

OBSERVATIONS *and* **SUPPOSITIONS,** *towards forming a new* **Hypothesis,** *for explaining the several* **Phænomena** *of* **Thunder-Gusts.**[6]

SIR,

§. 1. Non-electric bodies, that have electric fire thrown into them, will retain it ‹till other non-electrics, that have less, approach; and then ‹tis communicated by a snap, and becomes equally divided.

2. Electrical fire loves water, is strongly attracted by it, and they can subsist together.

3. Air is an electric *per se*, and when dry will not conduct the electrical fire; it will neither receive it, nor give it to other bodies; otherwise no body surrounded by air could be electrified positively and negatively: for should it be attempted positively, the air would immediately take away the overplus; or negatively, the air would supply what was wanting.

4. Water being electrified, the vapours arising from it will be equally electrified; and floating in the air, in the form of clouds, or otherwise, will retain that quantity of electrical fire, till they meet with other clouds or bodies not so much electrified, and then will communicate as beforementioned.

5. Every particle of matter electrified is repelled by every other particle equally electrified. Thus the stream of a fountain, naturally dense and continual, when electrified, will separate and spread in the form of a brush, every drop endeavouring to recede from every other drop. But on taking out the electrical fire, they close again.

6. Water being strongly electrified (as well as when heated by common fire) rises in vapours more copiously; the attraction of cohesion among its particles being greatly weakened, by the opposite power of repulsion introduced with the electrical fire; and when any particle is by any means disengaged, 'tis immediately repelled, and so flies into the air.

7. Particles happening to be situated as *A* and *B*, are more easily disengaged than *C* and *D*, as each is held by contact with three only, whereas *C* and *D* are each in contact with nine. When the surface of water has the least motion, particles are continually pushed into the situation represented by Fig. 6.

---

[6] Thunder-gusts are sudden storms of thunder and lightning, which are frequently of short duration, but sometimes produce mischievous effects.

8. Friction between a non-electric and an electric *per se*, will produce electrical fire; not by *creating*, but *collecting* it: for it is equally diffused in our walls, floors, earth, and the whole mass of common matter. Thus the whirling glass globe, during its friction against the cushion, draws fire from the cushion, the cushion is supplied from the frame of the machine, that from the floor on which it stands. Cut off the communication by thick glass or wax placed under the cushion, and no fire can be *produced*, because it cannot be *collected*.

9. The Ocean is a compound of water, a non-electric, and salt an electric *per se*.

10. When there is a friction among the parts near its surface, the electrical fire is collected from the parts below. It is then plainly visible in the night; it appears at the stern and in the wake of every sailing vessel; every dash of an oar shows it, and every surff and spray: in storms the whole sea seems on fire.—The detach'd particles of water then repelled from the electrified surface, continually carry off the fire as it is collected; they rise, and form clouds, and those clouds are highly electrified, and retain the fire 'till they have an opportunity of communicating it.

11. The particles of water rising in vapours, attach themselves to particles of air.

12. The particles of air are said to be hard, round, separate and distant from each other; every particle strongly repelling every other particle, whereby they recede from each other, as far as common gravity will permit.

13. The space between any three particles equally repelling each other, will be an equilateral triangle.

14. In air compressed, these triangles are smaller; in rarified Air they are larger.

15. Common fire joined with air, increases the repulsion, enlarges the triangles, and thereby makes the air specifically lighter. Such Air among denser air, will rise.

16. Common fire, as well as electrical fire gives repulsion to the particles of water, and destroys their attraction of cohesion; hence common fire, as well as electrical fire, assists in raising vapours.

17. Particles of water, having no fire in them, mutually attract each other. Three particles of water then being attached to the three particles of a triangle of air, would by their mutual attraction operating against the air's repulsion, shorten the sides and lessen the triangle, whereby that portion of air being made denser, would sink to the earth with its water, and not rise to contribute to the formation of a cloud.

18. But if every particle of water attaching itself to air, brings with it a particle of common fire, the repulsion of the air being assisted and strengthened by the fire, more than obstructed by the mutual attraction of the particles of water, the triangle dilates, and that portion of air becoming rarer and specifically lighter rises.

19. If the particles of water bring electrical fire when they attach themselves to air, the repulsion between the particles of water electrified, joins with the natural repulsion of the air, to force its particles to a greater distance, whereby the trian-

gles are dilated, and the air rises, carrying up with it the water.

20. If the particles of water bring with them portions of *both sorts* of fire, the repulsions of the particles of air is still more strengthened and increased, and the triangles farther enlarged.

21. One particle of air may be surrounded by twelve particles of water of equal size with itself, all in contact with it; and by more added to those.

22. Particles of air thus loaded would be drawn nearer together by the mutual attraction of the particles of water, did not the fire, common or electrical, assist their repulsion.

23. If air thus loaded be compressed by adverse winds, or by being driven against mountains, &c. or condensed by taking away the fire that assisted it in expanding; the triangles contract, the air with its water will descend as a dew; or, if the water surrounding one particle of air comes in contact with the water surrounding another, they coalesce and form a drop, and we have rain.

24. The sun supplies (or seems to supply) common fire to all vapours, whether raised from earth or sea.

25. Those vapours which have both common and electrical fire in them, are better supported, than those which have only common fire in them. For when vapours rise into the coldest region above the earth, the cold will not diminish the electrical fire, if it doth the common.

26. Hence clouds formed by vapours raised from fresh waters within land, from growing vegetables, moist earth, &c. more speedily and easily deposite their water, having but little electrical fire to repel and keep the particles separate. So that the greatest part of the water raised from the land is let fall on the land again; and winds blowing from the land to the sea are dry; there being little use for rain on the sea, and to rob the land of its moisture, in order to rain on the sea, would not appear reasonable.

27. But clouds formed by vapours raised from the sea, having both fires, and particularly a great quantity of the electrical, support their water strongly, raise it high, and being moved by winds may bring it over the middle of the broadest continent from the middle of the widest ocean.

28. How these ocean clouds, so strongly supporting their water, are made to deposite it on the land where 'tis wanted, is next to be considered.

29. If they are driven by winds against mountains, those mountains being less electrified attract them, and on contact take away their electrical fire (and being cold, the common fire also;) hence the particles close towards the mountains and towards each other. If the air was not much loaded, it only falls in dews on the mountain tops and sides, forms springs, and descends to the vales in rivulets, which united make larger streams and rivers. If much loaded, the electrical fire is at once taken from the whole cloud; and, in leaving it, flashes brightly and cracks loudly; the particles instantly coalescing for want of that fire, and falling in a heavy shower.

30. When a ridge of mountains thus dams the clouds, and draws the electrical fire from the cloud first approaching it; that which next follows, when it comes near the first cloud, now deprived of its fire, flashes into it, and begins to deposite its own water; the first cloud again flashing into the mountains; the third approaching cloud, and all the succeeding ones, acting in the same manner as far back as they extend, which may be over many hundred miles of country.

31. Hence the continual storms of rain, thunder, and lightning on the east-side of the *Andes*, which running north and south, and being vastly high, intercept all the clouds brought against them from the *Atlantic* ocean by the trade winds, and oblige them to deposite their waters, by which the vast rivers *Amazons*, *La Plata*, and *Oroonoko* are formed, which return the water into the same sea, after having fertilized a country of very great extent.

32. If a country be plain, having no mountains to intercept the electrified clouds, yet is it not without means to make them deposite their water. For if an electrified cloud coming from the sea, meets in the air a cloud raised from the land, and therefore not electrified; the first will flash its fire into the latter, and thereby both clouds shall be made suddenly to deposite water.

33. The electrified particles of the first cloud close when they lose their fire; the particles of the other cloud close in receiving it: in both, they have thereby an opportunity of coalescing into drops.—The concussion or jerk given to the air, contributes also to shake down the water, not only from those two clouds but from others near them. Hence the sudden fall of rain immediately after flashes of lightning.

34. To shew this by an easy experiment. Take two round pieces of pasteboard two inches diameter; from the center and circumference of each of them suspend by fine silk threads eighteen inches long, seven small balls of wood, or seven peas equal in bigness; so will the balls appending to each pasteboard, form equal equilateral triangles, one ball being in the center, and six at equal distances from that, and from each other; and thus they represent particles of air. Dip both sets in water, and some cohering to each ball they will represent air loaded. Dexterously electrify one set, and its balls will repel each other to a greater distance, enlarging the triangles. Could the water supported by the seven balls come into contact, it would form a drop or drops so heavy as to break the cohesion it had with the balls, and so fall.—Let the two sets then represent two clouds, the one a sea cloud electrified, the other a land cloud. Bring them within the sphere of attraction, and they will draw towards each other, and you will see the separated balls close thus; the first electrified ball that comes near an unelectrified ball by attraction joins it, and gives it fire; instantly they separate, and each flies to another ball of its own party, one to give, the other to receive fire; and so it proceeds through both sets, but so quick as to be in a manner instantaneous. In the collision they shake off and drop their water, which represents rain.

35. Thus when sea and land clouds would pass at too great a distance for the flash, they are attracted towards each other till within that distance; for the sphere of electrical attraction is far beyond the distance of flashing.

36. When a great number of clouds from the sea meet a number of clouds raised from the land, the electrical flashes appear to strike in different parts; and as the clouds are jostled and mixed by the winds, or brought near by the electrical attraction, they continue to give and receive flash after flash, till the electrical fire is equally diffused.

37. When the gun-barrel (in electrical experiments) has but little electrical fire in it, you must approach it very near with your knuckle, before you can draw a spark. Give it more fire, and it will give a spark at a greater distance. Two gun-barrels united, and as highly electrified, will give a spark at a still greater distance. But if two gun-barrels electrified will strike at two inches distance, and make a loud snap, to what a great distance may 10,000 acres of electrified cloud strike and give its fire, and how loud must be that crack!

38. It is a common thing to see clouds at different heights passing different ways, which shews different currents of air, one under the other. As the air between the tropics is rarified by the sun, it rises, the denser northern and southern air pressing into its place. The air so rarified and forced up, passes northward and southward, and must descend in the polar regions, if it has no opportunity before, that the circulation may be carried on.

39. As currents of air, with the clouds therein, pass different ways, 'tis easy to conceive how the clouds, passing over each other, may attract each other, and so come near enough for the electrical stroke. And also how electrical clouds may be carried within land very far from the sea, before they have an opportunity to strike.

40. When the air, with its vapours raised from the ocean between the tropics, comes to descend in the polar regions, and to be in contact with the vapours arising there, the electrical fire they brought begins to be communicated, and is seen in clear nights, being first visible where 'tis first in motion, that is, where the contact begins, or in the most northern part; from thence the streams of light seem to shoot southerly, even up to the zenith of northern countries. But tho' the light seems to shoot from the north southerly, the progress of the fire is really from the south northerly, its motion beginning in the north being the reason that 'tis there first seen.

For the electrical fire is never visible but when in motion, and leaping from body to body, or from particle to particle thro' the air. When it passes thro' dense bodies 'tis unseen. When a wire makes part of the circle, in the explosion of the electrical phial, the fire, though in great quantity, passes in the wire invisibly: but in passing along a chain, it becomes visible as it leaps from link to link. In passing along leaf-gilding 'tis visible: for the leaf-gold is full of pores; hold a leaf to the light and it appears like a net; and the fire is seen in its leaping over the vacancies.— And as when a long canal filled with still water is opened at one end, in order to be discharged, the motion of the water begins first near the opened end, and proceeds towards the close end, tho' the water itself moves from the close towards the opened end: so the electrical fire discharged into the polar regions, perhaps from a thousand leagues length of vaporiz'd air, appears first where 'tis first in motion, *i.*

e. in the most northern part, and the appearance proceeds southward, tho' the fire really moves northward. This is supposed to account for the *Aurora Borealis*.

41. When there is great heat on the land, in a particular region (the sun having shone on it perhaps several days, while the surrounding countries have been screen'd by clouds) the lower air is rarified and rises, the cooler denser air above descends; the clouds in that air meet from all sides, and join over the heated place; and if some are electrified, others not, lightning and thunder succeed, and showers fall. Hence thunder-gusts after heats, and cool air after gusts; the water and the clouds that bring it, coming from a higher and therefore a cooler region.

42. An electrical spark, drawn from an irregular body at some distance is scarce ever strait, but shows crooked and waving in the air. So do the flashes of lightning; the clouds being very irregular bodies.

43. As electrified clouds pass over a country, high hills and high trees, lofty towers, spires, masts of ships, chimneys, *&c.* as so many prominencies and points, draw the electrical fire, and the whole cloud discharges there.

44. Dangerous, therefore, is it to take shelter under a tree during a thunder-gust. It has been fatal to many, both men and beasts.

45. It is safer to be in the open field for another reason. When the clothes are wet, if a flash in its way to the ground should strike your head, it will run in the water over the surface of your body; whereas, if your clothes were dry, it would go thro' the body.

Hence a wet rat cannot be killed by the exploding electrical bottle, when a dry rat may.

46. Common fire is in all bodies, more or less, as well as electrical fire. Perhaps they may be different modifications of the same element; or they may be different elements. The latter is by some suspected.

47. If they are different things, yet they may and do subsist together in the same body.

48. When electrical fire strikes thro' a body, it acts upon the common fire contained in it, and puts that fire in motion; and if there be a sufficient quantity of each kind of fire, the body will be inflamed.

49. When the quantity of common fire in the body is small, the quantity of the electrical fire (or the electrical stroke) should be greater: if the quantity of common fire be great, less electrical fire suffices to produce the effect.

50. Thus spirits must be heated before we can fire them by the electrical spark. If they are much heated a small spark will do; if not, the spark must be greater.

51. Till lately we could only fire warm vapours; but now we can burn hard dry rosin. And when we can procure greater electrical sparks, we may be able to fire not only unwarm'd spirits, as lightning does, but even wood, by giving sufficient agitation to the common fire contained in it, as friction we know will do.

52. Sulphureous and inflammable vapours arising from the earth, are easily

kindled by lightning. Besides what arise from the earth, such vapours are sent out by stacks of moist hay, corn, or other vegetables, which heat and reek. Wood rotting in old trees or buildings does the same. Such are therefore easily and often fired.

53. Metals are often melted by lightning, tho' perhaps not from heat in the lightning, nor altogether from agitated fire in the metals.—For as whatever body can insinuate itself between the particles of metal, and overcome the attraction by which they cohere (as sundry menstrua can) will make the solid become a fluid, as well as fire, yet without heating it: so the electrical fire, or lightning, creating a violent repulsion between the particles of the metal it passes thro', the metal is fused.

54. If you would, by a violent fire, melt off the end of a nail, which is half driven into a door, the heat given the whole nail before a part would melt, must burn the board it sticks in. And the melted part would burn the floor it dropp'd on. But if a sword can be melted in the scabbard, and money in a man's pocket, by lightning, without burning either, it must be a cold fusion.

55. Lightning rends some bodies. The electrical spark will strike a hole thro' a quire of strong paper.

56. If the source of lightning, assigned in this paper, be the true one, there should be little thunder heard at sea far from land. And accordingly some old sea-captains, of whom enquiry has been made, do affirm, that the fact agrees perfectly with the hypothesis; for that, in crossing the great ocean, they seldom meet with thunder till they come into soundings; and that the islands far from the continent have very little of it. And a curious observer, who lived 13 years at *Bermudas,* says, there was less thunder there in that whole time than he has sometimes heard in a month at *Carolina.*

ADDITIONAL PAPERS.

TO
MR. PETER COLLINSON, F.R.S. LONDON.

Philadelphia, July 29, 1750

SIR,

As you first put us on electrical experiments, by sending to our library company a tube, with directions how to use it; and as our honourable proprietary enabled us to carry those experiments to a greater height, by his generous present of a compleat electrical apparatus; 'tis fit that both should know from time to time what progress we make. It was in this view I wrote and sent you my former papers on this subject, desiring, that as I had not the honour of a direct correspondence with that bountiful benefactor to our library, they might be communicated to him through your hands. In the same view I write, and send you this additional paper. If it happens to bring you nothing new (which may well be, considering the number of ingenious men in *Europe*, continually engaged in the same researches) at least it will show, that the instruments, put into our hands, are not neglected; and, that if no valuable discoveries are made by us, whatever the cause may be, it is not want of industry and application.

I am, Sir,
Your much obliged
Humble Servant,
B. FRANKLIN.

OPINIONS and CONJECTURES,
Concerning the Properties and Effects of the electrical Matter, arising
from Experiments and Observations, made in Philadelphia, 1749.

§ 1. The electrical matter consists of particles extreamly subtile, since it can permeate common matter, even the densest metals, with such ease and freedom, as not to receive any perceptible resistance.

2. If any one should doubt, whether the electrical matter passes thro' the substance of bodies, or only over and along their surfaces, a shock from an electrified large glass jar, taken thro' his own body, will probably convince him.

3. Electrical matter differs from common matter in this, that the parts of the latter mutually attract, those of the former mutually repel, each other. Hence the appearing divergency in a stream of electrified effluvia.

4. But tho' the particles of electrical matter do repel each other, they are strongly attracted by all other matter.[7]

5. From these three things, the extreme subtilty of the electrical matter, the mutual repulsion of its parts, and the strong attraction between them and other matter, arise this effect, that when a quantity of electrical matter, is applied to a mass of common matter, of any bigness or length within our observation (which has not already got its quantity) it is immediately and equally diffused through the whole.

6. Thus common matter is a kind of spunge to the electrical fluid. And as a spunge would receive no water, if the parts of water were not smaller than the pores of the spunge; and even then but slowly, if there were not a mutual attraction between those parts and the parts of the spunge; and would still imbibe it faster, if the mutual attraction among the parts of the water did not impede, some force being required to separate them; and fastest, if, instead of attraction, there were a mutual repulsion among those parts, which would act in conjunction with the attraction of the spunge. So is the case between the electrical and common matter.

7. But in common matter there is (generally) as much of the electrical, as it will contain within its substance. If more is added, it lies without upon the surface, and forms what we call an electrical atmosphere: and then the body is said to be electrified.

8. 'Tis supposed, that all kinds of common matter do not attract and retain the electrical, with equal strength and force; for reasons to be given hereafter. And that those called electrics *per se*, as glass, &c. attract and retain it strongest, and contain the greatest quantity.

9. We know that the electrical fluid is *in* common matter, because we can pump it *out* by the globe or tube. We know that common matter has near as much as it can contain, because, when we add a little more to any protion of it, the additional quantity does not enter, but forms an electrical atmosphere. And we know that common matter has not (generally) more than it can contain, otherwise all loose portions of it would repel each other, as they constantly do when they have electric atmospheres.

10. The beneficial uses of this electrical fluid in the creation, we are not yet well acquainted with, though doubtless such there are, and those very considerable; but we may see some pernicious consequences, that would attend a much greater proportion of it. For had this globe we live on as much of it in proportion, as we can give to a globe of iron, wood, or the like, the particles of dust and other light matters that get loose from it, would, by virtue of their separate electrical atmospheres, not only repel each other, but be repelled from the earth, and not easily be brought to unite with it again; whence our air would continually be more and more clogged with foreign matter, and grow unfit for respiration. This affords another occasion of adoring that wisdom which has made all things by weight and measure!

11. If a piece of common matter be supposed intirely free from electrical matter, and a single particle of the latter be brought nigh, 'twill be attracted and enter

[7] See the ingenious essays on electricity in the Transactions, by Mr Ellicot.

the body, and take place in the center, or where the attraction is every way equal. If more particles enter, they take their places where the balance is equal between the attraction of the common matter and their own mutual repulsion. 'Tis supposed they form triangles, whose sides shorten as their number increases; 'till the common matter has drawn in so many, that its whole power of compressing those triangles by attraction, is equal to their whole power of expanding themselves by repulsion; and then will such piece of matter receive no more.

12. When part of this natural proportion of electrical fluid, is taken out of a piece of common matter, the triangles formed by the remainder, are supposed to widen by the mutual repulsion of the parts, until they occupy the whole piece.

13. When the quantity of electrical fluid taken from a piece of common matter is restored again, it enters, the expanded triangles being again compressed till there is room for the whole.

14. To explain this: take two apples, or two balls of wood or other matter, each having its own natural quantity of the electrical fluid. Suspend them by silk lines from the ceiling. Apply the wire of a well-charged vial, held in your hand, to one of them (A) Fig. 7. and it will receive from the wire a quantity of the electrical fluid; but will not imbibe it, being already full. The fluid therefore will flow round its surface, and form an electrical atmosphere. Bring A into contact with B, and half the electrical fluid is communicated, so that each has now an electrical atmosphere, and therefore they repel each other. Take away these atmospheres by touching the balls, and leave them in their natural state: then, having fixed a stick of sealing wax to the middle of the vial to hold it by, apply the wire to A, at the same time the coating touches B. Thus will a quantity of the electrical fluid be drawn out of B, and thrown on A. So that A will have a redundance of this fluid, which forms an atmosphere round it, and B an exactly equal deficiency. Now bring these balls again into contact, and the electrical atmosphere will not be divided between A and B, into two smaller atmospheres as before; for B will drink up the whole atmosphere of A, and both will be found again in their natural state.

15. The form of the electrical atmosphere is that of the body it surrounds. This shape may be rendered visible in a still air, by raising a smoke from dry rosin, dropt into a hot tea-spoon under the electrised body, which will be attracted and spread itself equaly on all sides, covering and concealing the body. And this form it takes, because it is attracted by all parts of the surface of the body, tho' it cannot enter the substance already replete. Without this attraction it would not remain round the body, but dissipate in the air.

16. The atmosphere of electrical particles surrounding an electrified sphere, is not more disposed to leave it or more easily drawn off from any one part of the sphere than from another, because it is equally attracted by every part. But that is not the case with bodies of any other figure. From a cube it is more easily drawn at the corners than at the plane sides, and so from the angles of a body of any other form, and still most easily from the angle that is most acute. Thus if a body shaped as A, B, C, D, E, in Fig. 8, be electrified, or have an electrical atmosphere communicated to it, and we consider every side as a base on which the particles

rest and by which they are attracted, one may see, by imagining a line from A to F, and another from E to G, that the portion of the atmosphere included in F, A, E, G, has the line A, E, for its basis. So the portion of atmosphere included in H, A, B, I, has the line A, B, for its basis. And likewise the portion included in K, B, C, L, has B, C, to rest on; and so on the other side of the figure. Now if you would draw off this atmosphere with any blunt smooth body, and approach the middle of the side A, B, you must come very near before the force of your attracter exceeds the force or power with which that side holds its atmosphere. But there is a small portion between I, B, K, that has less of the surface to rest on, and to be attracted by, than the neighbouring portions, while at the same time there is a mutual repulsion between its particles and the particles of those portions, therefore here you can get it with more ease or at a greater distance. Between F, A, H, there is a larger portion that has yet a less surface to rest on and to attract it; here therefore you can get it away still more easily. But easiest of all between L, C, M, where the quantity is largest, and the surface to attract and keep it back the least. When you have drawn away one of these angular portions of the fluid, another succeeds in its place, from the nature of fluidity and the mutual repulsion beforementioned; and so the atmosphere continues flowing off at such angle, like a stream, till no more is remaining. The extremities of the portions of atmosphere over these angular parts are likewise at a greater distance from the electrified body, as may be seen by the inspection of the above figure; the point of the atmosphere of the angle C, being much farther from C, than any other part of the atmosphere over the lines C, B, or B, A: And besides the distance arising from the nature of the figure, where the attraction is less, the particles will naturally expand to a greater distance by their mutual repulsion. On these accounts we suppose electrified bodies discharge their atmospheres upon unelectrified bodies more easily and at a greater distance from their angles and points than from their smooth sides.—Those points will also discharge into the air, when the body has too great an electrical atmosphere, without bringing any non-electric near, to receive what is thrown off: For the air, though an electric *per se*, yet has always more or less water and other non-electric matters mixed with it; and these attract and receive what is so discharged.

17. But points have a property, by which they *draw on* as well as *throw off* the electrical fluid, at greater distances than blunt bodies can. That is, as the pointed part of an electrified body will discharge the atmosphere of that body, or communicate it farthest to another body, so the point of an unelectrified body, will draw off the electrical atmosphere from an electrified body, farther than a blunter part of the same unelectrified body will do. Thus a pin held by the head, and the point presented to an electrified body, will draw off its atmosphere at a foot distance; where if the head were presented instead of the point, no such effect would follow. To understand this, we may consider, that if a person standing on the floor would draw off the electrical atmosphere from an electrified body, an iron crow and a blunt knitting kneedle held alternately in his hand and presented for that purpose, do not draw with different forces in proportion to their different masses. For the man, and what he holds in his hand, be it large or small, are connected with the common mass of unelectrified matter; and the force with which he draws is the same in both cases, it consisting in the different proportion of electricity in the

electrified body and that common mass. But the force with which the electrified body retains its atmosphere by attracting it, is proportioned to the surface over which the particles are placed; i.e. four square inches of that surface retain their atmosphere with four times the force that one square inch retains its atmosphere. And as in plucking the hairs from the horse's tail, a degree of strength insufficient to pull away a handful at once, could yet easily strip it hair by hair; so a blunt body presented cannot draw off a number of particles at once, but a pointed one, with no greater force, takes them away easily, particle by particle.

18. These explanations of the power and operation of points, when they first occurr'd to me, and while they first floated in my mind, appeared perfectly satisfactory; but now I have wrote them, and consider'd them more closely in black and white, I must own I have some doubts about them: yet as I have at present nothing better to offer in their stead, I do not cross them out: for even a bad solution read, and its faults discover'd, has often given rise to a good one in the mind of an ingenious reader.

19. Nor is it of much importance to us, to know the manner in which nature executes her laws; 'tis enough if we know the laws themselves. 'Tis of real use to know, that china left in the air unsupported will fall and break; but *how* it comes to fall, and *why* it breaks, are matters of speculation. 'Tis a pleasure indeed to know them, but we can preserve our china without it.

20. Thus in the present case, to know this power of points, may possibly be of some use to mankind, though we should never be able to explain it. The following experiments, as well as those in my first paper, show this power. I have a large prime conductor made of several thin sheets of Fuller's pasteboard form'd into a tube, near 10 feet long and a foot diameter. It is cover'd with *Dutch* emboss'd paper, almost totally gilt. This large metallic surface supports a much greater electrical atmosphere than a rod of iron of 50 times the weight would do. It is suspended by silk lines, and when charg'd will strike at near two inches distance, a pretty hard stroke so as to make one's knuckle ach. Let a person standing on the floor present the point of a needle at 12 or more inches distance from it, and while the needle is so presented, the conductor cannot be charged, the point drawing off the fire as fast as it is thrown on by the electrical globe. Let it be charged, and then present the point at the same distance, and it will suddenly be discharged. In the dark you may see a light on the point, when the experiment is made. And if the person holding the point stands upon wax, he will be electrified by receiving the fire at that distance. Attempt to draw off the electricity with a blunt body, as a bolt of iron round at the end and smooth (a silversmith's iron punch, inch-thick, is what I use) and you must bring it within the distance of three inches before you can do it, and then it is done with a stroke and crack. As the pasteboard tube hangs loose on silk lines, when you approach it with the punch iron, it likewise will move towards the punch, being attracted while it is charged; but if at the same instant a point be presented as before, it retires again, for the point discharges it. Take a pair of large brass scales, of two or more feet beam, the cords of the scales being silk. Suspend the beam by a packthread from the cieling, so that the bottom of the scales may be about a foot from the floor: The scales will move round in a circle by the untwist-

ing of the packthread. Set the iron punch on the end upon the floor, in such a place as that the scales may pass over it in making their circle: Then electrify one scale by applying the wire of a charged phial to it. As they move round, you see that scale draw nigher to the floor, and dip more when it comes over the punch; and if that be placed at a proper distance, the scale will snap and discharge its fire into it. But if a needle be stuck on the end of the punch, its point upwards, the scale, instead of drawing nigh to the punch and snapping, discharges its fire silently through the point, and rises higher from the punch. Nay, even if the needle be placed upon the floor near the punch, its point upwards, the end of the punch, tho' so much higher than the needle, will not attract the scale and receive its fire, for the needle will get it and convey it away, before it comes nigh enough for the punch to act. And this is constantly observable in these experiments, that the greater quantity of electricity on the pasteboard tube, the farther it strikes or discharges its fire, and the point likewise will draw it off at a still greater distance.

Now if the fire of electricity and that of lightening be the same, as I have endeavour'd to show at large in a former paper, this pasteboard tube and these scales may represent electrified clouds. If a tube of only 10 feet long will strike and discharge its fire on the punch at two or three inches distance, an electrified cloud of perhaps 10,000 acres, may strike and discharge on the earth at a proportionably greater distance. The horizontal motion of the scales over the floor, may represent the motion of the clouds over the earth; and the erect iron punch, a hill or high building; and then we see how electrified clouds passing over hills or high buildings at too great a height to strike, may be attracted lower till within their striking distance. And lastly, if a needle fix'd on the punch with its point upright, or even on the floor below the punch, will draw the fire from the scale silently at a much greater than the striking distance, and so prevent its descending towards the punch; or if in its course it would have come nigh enough to strike, yet being first deprived of its fire it cannot, and the punch is thereby secured from the stroke. I say, if these things are so, may not the knowledge of this power of points be of use to mankind, in preserving houses, churches, ships, &c. from the stroke of lightning, by directing us to fix on the highest parts of those edifices, upright rods of iron made sharp as a needle, and gilt to prevent rusting, and from the foot of those rods a wire down the outside of the building into the ground, or down round one of the shrouds of a ship, and down her side till it reaches the water? Would not these pointed rods probably draw the electrical fire silently out of a cloud before it came nigh enough to strike, and thereby secure us from that most sudden and terrible mischief?

21. To determine the question, whether the clouds that contain lightning are electrified or not, I would propose an experiment to be try'd where it may be done conveniently. On the top of some high tower or steeple, place a kind of sentry-box, (as in Fig. 9.) big enough to contain a man and an electrical stand. From the middle of the stand, let an iron rod rise and pass bending out of the door, and then upright 20 or 30 feet, pointed very sharp at the end. If the electrical stand be kept clean and dry, a man standing on it when such clouds are passing low, might be electrified and afford sparks, the rod drawing fire to him from a cloud. If any danger to the

man should be apprehended (though I think there would be none) let him stand on the floor of his box, and now and then bring near to the rod, the loop of a wire that has one end fastened to the leads, he holding it by a wax handle; so the sparks, if the rod is electrified, will strike from the rod to the wire, and not affect him.

22. Before I leave this subject of lightning, I may mention some other similarities between the effects of that, and these of electricity. Lightning has often been known to strike people blind. A pigeon that we struck dead to appearance by the electrical shock, recovering life, droop'd about the yard several days, eat nothing though crumbs were thrown to it, but declined and died. We did not think of its being deprived of sight; but afterwards a pullet struck dead in like manner, being recovered by repeatedly blowing into its lungs, when set down on the floor, ran headlong against the wall, and on examination appeared perfectly blind. Hence we concluded that the pigeon also had been absolutely blinded by the shock. The biggest animal we have yet killed or try'd to kill with the electrical stroke, was a well-grown pullet.

23. Reading in the ingenious Dr. *Hales*'s account of the thunder storm at *Stretham*, the effect of the lightning in stripping off all the paint that had covered a gilt moulding of a pannel of wainscot, without hurting the rest of the paint, I had a mind to lay a coat of paint over the filleting of gold on the cover of a book, and try the effect of a strong electrical flash sent through that gold from a charged sheet of glass. But having no paint at hand, I pasted a narrow strip of paper over it; and when dry, sent the flash through the gilding; by which the paper was torn off from end to end, with such force, that it was broke in several places, and in others brought away part of the grain of the Turky-leather in which it was bound; and convinced me, that had it been painted, the paint would have been stript off in the same manner with that on the wainscot at *Stretham*.

24. Lightning melts metals, and I hinted in my paper on that subject, that I suspected it to be a cold fusion; I do not mean a fusion by force of cold, but a fusion without heat. We have also melted gold, silver, and copper, in small quantities, by the electrical flash. The manner is this: Take leaf gold, leaf silver, or leaf gilt copper, commonly called leaf brass or *Dutch* gold: cut off from the leaf long narrow strips the breadth of a straw. Place one of these strips between two strips of smooth glass that are about the width of your finger. If one strip of gold, the length of the leaf, be not long enough for the glass, add another to the end of it, so that you may have a little part hanging out loose at each end of the glass. Bind the pieces of glass together from end to end with strong silk thread; then place it so as to be part of an electrical circle, (the ends of gold hanging out being of use to join with the other parts of the circle) and send the flash through it, from a large electrified jar or sheet of glass. Then if your strips of glass remain whole, you will see that the gold is missing in several places, and instead of it a metallic stain on both the glasses; the stains on the upper and under glass exactly similar in the minutest stroke, as may be seen by holding them to the light; the metal appeared to have been not only melted, but even vitrified, or otherwise so driven into the pores of the glass, as to be protected by it from the action of the strongest *Aqua Fortis* and *Ag: Regia*. I send you enclosed two little pieces of glass with these metallic stains upon them,

which cannot be removed without taking part of the glass with them. Sometimes the stain spreads a little wider than the breadth of the leaf, and looks brighter at the edge, as by inspecting closely you may observe in these. Sometimes the glass breaks to pieces: once the upper glass broke into a thousand pieces, looking like coarse salt. These pieces I send you, were stain'd with *Dutch* gold. True gold makes a darker stain, somewhat reddish; silver, a greenish stain. We once took two pieces of thick looking-glass, as broad as a Gunter's scale, and 6 inches long; and placing leaf gold between them, put them betwixt two smoothly plain'd pieces of wood, and fix'd them tight in a book-binder's small press; yet though they were so closely confined, the force of the electrical shock shivered the glass into many pieces. The gold was melted and stain'd into the glass as usual. The circumstances of the breaking of the glass differ much in making the experiment, and sometimes it does not break at all: but this is constant, that the stains in the upper and under pieces are exact counterparts of each other. And though I have taken up the pieces of glass between my fingers immediately after this melting, I never could perceive the least warmth in them.

25. In one of my former papers, I mention'd, that gilding on a book, though at first it communicated the shock perfectly well, yet fail'd after a few experiments, which we could not account for. We have since found, that one strong shock breaks the continuity of the gold in the filleting, and makes it look rather like dust of gold, abundance of its parts being broken and driven off; and it will seldom conduct above one strong shock. Perhaps this may be the reason; when there is not a perfect continuity in the circle, the fire must leap over the vacancies; there is a certain distance which it is able to leap over according to its strength; if a number of small vacancies, though each be very minute, taken together exceed that distance, it cannot leap over them, and so the shock is prevented.

26. From the before mentioned law of electricity, that points, as they are more or less acute, draw on and throw off the electrical fluid with more or less power, and at greater or less distances, and in larger or smaller quantities in the same time, we may see how to account for the situation of the leaf of gold suspended between two plates, the upper one continually electrified, the under one in a person's hand standing on the floor. When the upper plate is electrified, the leaf is attracted and raised towards it, and would fly to that plate were it not for its own points. The corner that happens to be uppermost when the leaf is rising, being a sharp point, from the extream thinness of the gold, draws and receives at a distance a sufficient quantity of the electrical fluid to give itself an electrical atmosphere, by which its progress to the upper plate is stopt, and it begins to be repelled from that plate, and would be driven back to the under plate, but that its lowest corner is likewise a point, and throws off or discharges the overplus of the leaf's atmosphere, as fast as the upper corner draws it on. Were these two points perfectly equal in acuteness, the leaf would take place exactly in the middle space, for its Weight is a trifle, compared to the power acting on it: But it is generally nearest the unelectrified plate, because, when the leaf is offered to the electrified plate at a distance, the sharpest point is commonly first affected and raised towards it; so that point, from its greater acuteness, receiving the fluid faster than its opposite can discharge

it at equal distances, it retires from the electrified plate, and draws nearer to the unelectrified plate, till it comes to a distance where the discharge can be exactly equal to the receipt, the latter being lessened, and the former encreased; and there it remains as long as the globe continues to supply fresh electrical matter. This will appear plain, when the difference of acuteness in the corners is made very great. Cut a piece of *Dutch* gold (which is fittest for these experiments on account of its greater strength) into the form of Fig. 10 the upper corner a right angle, the two next obtuse angles, and the lowest a very acute one; and bring this on your plate under the electrified plate, in such a manner as that the right-angled part may be first raised (which is done by covering the acute part with the hollow of your hand) and you will see this leaf take place much nearer to the upper than to the under plate; because, without being nearer, it cannot receive so fast at its right-angled point, as it can discharge at its acute one. Turn this leaf with the acute part uppermost, and then it takes place nearest the unelectrified plate, because otherwise it receives faster at its acute point than it can discharge at its right-angled one. Thus the difference of distance is always proportioned to the difference of acuteness. Take care in cutting your leaf to leave no little ragged particles on the edges, which sometimes form points where you would not have them. You may make this figure so acute below and blunt above, as to need no under plate, it discharging fast enough into the air. When it is made narrower, as the figure between the pricked lines, we call it the *Golden Fish*, from its manner of acting. For if you take it by the tail, and hold it at a foot or greater horizontal distance from the prime conductor, it will, when let go, fly to it with a brisk but wavering motion, like that of an eel through the water; it will then take place under the prime conductor, at perhaps a quarter or half an inch distance, and keep a continual shaking of its tail like a fish, so that it seems animated. Turn its tail towards the prime conductor, and then it flies to your finger, and seems to nibble it. And if you hold a plate under it at six or eight inches distance, and cease turning the Globe, when the electrical atmosphere of the conductor grows small, it will descend to the plate and swim back again several times with the same fish-like motion, greatly to the entertainment of spectators. By a little practice in blunting or sharpening the heads or tails of these figures, you may make them take place as desired, nearer, or farther from the electrified plate.

27. It is said in section 8, of this paper, that all kinds of common matter are supposed not to attract the electrical fluid with equal strength; and that those called electrics *per se*, as glass, &c. attract and retain it strongest, and contain the greatest quantity. This latter position may seem a paradox to some, being contrary to the hitherto received opinion; and therefore I shall now endeavour to explain it.

28. In order to this, let it first be considered, *that we cannot, by any means we are yet acquainted with, force the electrical fluid thro' glass.* I know it is commonly thought that it easily pervades glass, and the experiment of a feather suspended by a thread in a bottle hermetically sealed, yet moved by bringing a nibbed tube near the outside of the bottle, is alledged to prove it. But, if the electrical fluid so easily pervades glass, how does the vial become *charged* (as we term it) when we hold it in our hands? Would not the fire thrown in by the wire pass through to our hands, and so escape into the floor? Would not the bottle in that case be left just

as we found it, uncharged, as we know a metal bottle so attempted to be charged would be? Indeed, if there be the least crack, the minutest solution of continuity in the glass, though it remains so tight that nothing else we know of will pass, yet the extremely subtile electrical fluid flies through such a crack with the greatest freedom, and such a bottle we know can never be charged: What then makes the difference between such a bottle and one that is sound, but this, that the fluid can pass through the one, and not through the other?[8]

29. It is true there is an experiment that at first sight would be apt to satisfy a slight observer, that the fire thrown into the bottle by the wire, does really pass thro' the glass. It is this: place the bottle on a glass stand, under the prime conductor; suspend a bullet by a chain from the prime conductor, till it comes within a quarter of an inch right over the wire of the bottle; place your knuckle on the glass stand, at just the same distance from the coating of the bottle, as the bullet is from its wire. Now let the globe be turned, and you see a spark strike from the bullet to the wire of the bottle, and the same instant you see and feel an exactly equal spark striking from the coating on your knuckle, and so on spark for spark. This looks as if the whole received by the bottle was again discharged from it. And yet the bottle by this means is charged![9] And therefore the fire that thus leaves the bottle, though the same in quantity, cannot be the very same fire that entered at the wire; for if it were, the bottle would remain uncharged.

30. If the fire that so leaves the bottle be not the same that is thrown in through the wire, it must be fire that subsisted in the bottle, (that is, in the glass of the bottle) before the operation began.

31. If so, there must be a great quantity in glass, because a great quantity is thus discharged even from very thin glass.

32. That this electrical fluid or fire is strongly attracted by glass, we know from the quickness and violence with which it is resumed by the part that had been deprived of it, when there is an opportunity. And by this, that we cannot from a mass of glass draw a quantity of electrical fire, or electrify the whole mass *minus*, as we can a mass of metal. We cannot lessen or increase its whole quantity, for the quantity it has it holds; and it has as much as it can hold. Its pores are filled with it as full as the mutual repellency of the particles will admit; and what is already in, refuses, or strongly repels, any additional quantity. Nor have we any way of moving the electrical fluid in glass, but one; that is, by covering part of the two surfaces of thin glass with non-electrics, and then throwing an additional quantity of this fluid on one surface, which spreading in the non-electric, and being bound by it to that surface, acts by its repelling force on the particles of the electrical fluid contained in the other surface, and drives them out of the glass into the non-electric on that side, from whence they are discharged, and then those added on the charged side can enter. But when this is done, there is no more in the glass, nor less than before, just as much having left it on one side as it received on the other.

---

[8] See the first sixteen Sections of my former Paper, called *Farther Experiments*, &c.
[9] See § 10 of *Farther Experiments*, &c.

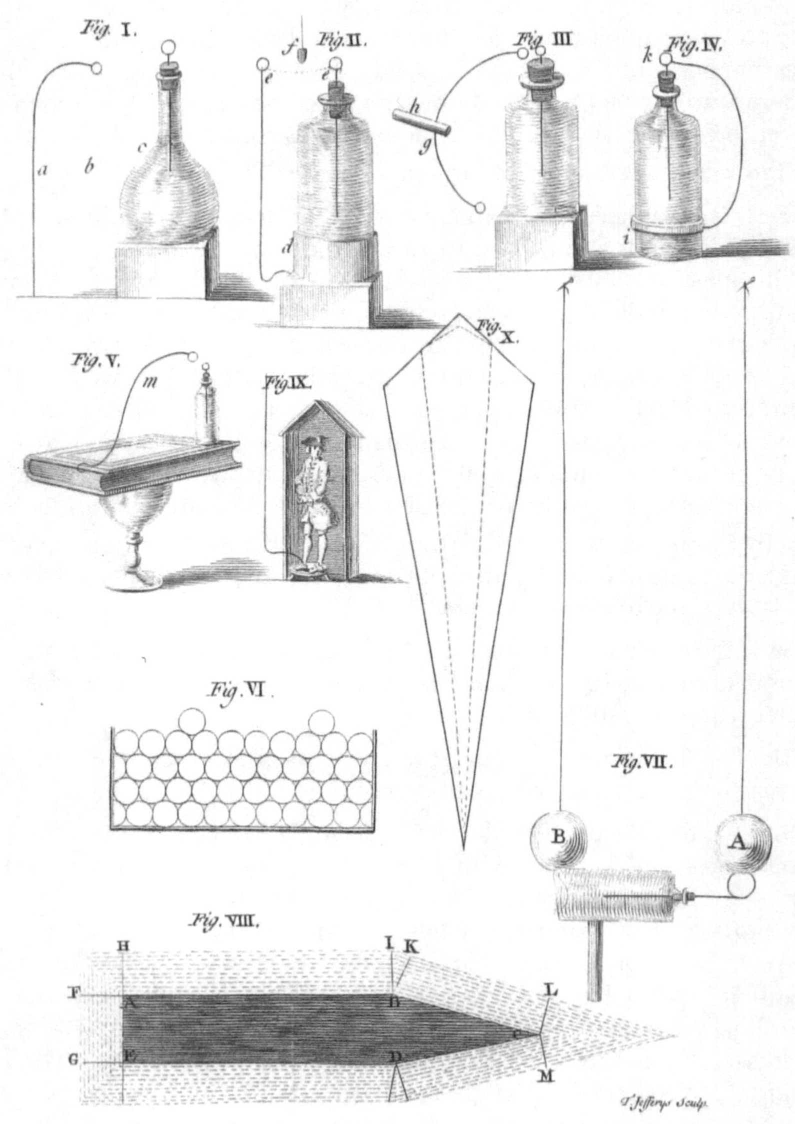

33. I feel a want of terms here, and doubt much whether I shall be able to make this part intelligible. By the word *surface*, in this case, I do not mean mere length and breadth without thickness; but when I speak of the upper or under surface of a piece of glass, the outer or inner surface of the vial, I mean length, breadth, and half the thickness, and beg the favour of being so understood. Now, I suppose, that glass in its first principles, and in the Furnace, has no more of this electrical fluid than other common matter: That when it is blown, as it cools, and the particles of common fire leave it, its pores become a vacuum: That the component parts

of glass are extremely small and fine, I guess from its never showing a rough face when it breaks, but always a polish; and from the smallness of its particles I suppose the pores between them must be exceeding small, which is the reason that Aqua-fortis, nor any other menstruum we have, can enter to separate them and dissolve the substance; nor is any fluid we know of, fine enough to enter, except common fire, and the electrical fluid. Now the departing fire leaving a vacuum, as aforesaid, between these pores, which air nor water are fine enough to enter and fill, the electrical fluid (which is every where ready in what we call the non-electrics, and in the non-electric Mixtures that are in the air,) is attracted in: yet does not become fixed with the substance of the glass, but subsists there as water in a porous stone, retained only by the attraction of the fixed parts, itself still loose and a fluid. But I suppose farther, that in the cooling of the glass, its texture becomes closest in the middle, and forms a kind of partition, in which the pores are so narrow, that the particles of the electrical fluid, which enter both surfaces at the same time, cannot go through, or pass and repass from one surface to the other, and so mix together; yet, though the particles of electrical fluid, imbibed by each surface, cannot themselves pass through to those of the other, their repellency can, and by this means they act on one another. The particles of the electrical fluid have a mutual repellency, but by the power of attraction in the glass they are condensed or forced nearer to each other. When the glass has received and, by its attraction, forced closer together so much of this electrified fluid, as that the power of attracting and condensing in the one, is equal to the power of expansion in the other, it can imbibe no more, and that remains its constant whole quantity; but each surface would receive more, if the repellency of what is in the opposite surface did not resist its entrance. The quantities of this fluid in each surface being equal, their repelling action on each other is equal; and therefore those of one surface cannot drive out those of the other: but, if a greater quantity is forced into one surface than the glass would naturally draw in; this increases the repelling power on that side, and overpowering the attraction on the other, drives out part of the fluid that had been imbibed by that surface, if there be any non-electric ready to receive it: such there is in all cases where glass is electrified to give a shock. The surface that has been thus emptied by having its electrical fluid driven out, resumes again an equal quantity with violence, as soon as the glass has an opportunity to discharge that over-quantity more than it could retain by attraction in its other surface, by the additional repellency of which the vacuum had been occasioned. For experiments favouring (if I may not say confirming) this hypothesis, I must, to avoid repetition, beg leave to refer you back to what is said of the electrical phial in my former papers.

34. Let us now see how it will account for several other appearances.—Glass, a body extremely elastic (and perhaps its elasticity may be owing in some degree to the subsisting of so great a quantity of this repelling fluid in its pores) must, when rubbed, have its rubbed surface somewhat stretched, or its solid parts drawn a little farther asunder, so that the vacancies in which the electrical fluid resides, become larger, affording room for more of that fluid, which is immediately attracted into it from the cushion or hand rubbing, they being supply'd from the common stock. But the instant the parts of the glass so open'd and fill'd have pass'd the friction,

they close again, and force the additional quantity out upon the surface, where it must rest till that part comes round to the cushion again, unless some non electric (as the prime conductor) first presents to receive it.[10] But if the inside of the globe be lined with a non-electric, the additional repellency of the electrical fluid, thus collected by friction on the rubb'd part of the globe's outer surface, drives an equal quantity out of the inner surface into that non-electric lining, which receiving it, and carrying it away from the rubb'd part into the common mass, through the axis of the globe and frame of the machine, the new collected electrical fluid can enter and remain in the outer surface, and none of it (or a very little) will be received by the prime conductor. As this charg'd part of the globe comes round to the cushion again, the outer surface delivers its overplus fire into the cushion, the opposite inner surface receiving at the same time an equal quantity from the floor. Every electrician knows that a globe wet within will afford little or no fire, but the reason has not before been attempted to be given, that I know of.

34. So if a tube lined with a[11]non-electric, be rubb'd, little or no fire is obtained from it. What is collected from the hand in the downward rubbing stroke, entering the pores of the glass, and driving an equal quantity out of the inner surface into the non-electric lining: and the hand in passing up to take a second stroke, takes out again what had been thrown into the outer surface, and then the inner surface receives back again what it had given to the non-electric lining. Thus the particles of electrical fluid belonging to the inside surface go in and out of their pores every stroke given to the tube. Put a wire into the tube, the inward end in contact with the non-electric lining, so it will represent the *Leyden* bottle. Let a second person touch the wire while you rub, and the fire driven out of the inward surface when you give the stroke, will pass through him into the common mass, and return through him when the inner surface resumes its quantity, and therefore this new kind of *Leyden* bottle cannot so be charged. But thus it may: after every stroke, before you pass your hand up to make another, let the second person apply his finger to the wire, take the spark, and then withdraw his finger; and so on till he has drawn a number of sparks; thus will the inner surface be exhausted, and the outer surface charged; then wrap a sheet of gilt paper close round the outer surface, and grasping it in your hand you may receive a shock by applying the finger of the other hand to the wire: for now the vacant pores in the inner surface resume their quantity, and the overcharg'd pores in the outer surface discharge that overplus; the equilibrium being restored through your body, which could not be restored through the glass.[12] If the tube be exhausted of air, a non electric lining in contact with the wire is not necessary; for *in vacuo*, the electrical fire will fly freely from the inner surface, without a non-electric conductor: but air resists its motion; for being itself an electric *per se*, it does not attract it, having already its quantity. So

---

[10] In the dark the electrical fluid may be seen on the cushion in two semi-circles or half-moons, one on the fore part, the other on the back part of the cushion, just where the globe and cushion separate. In the fore crescent the fire is passing out of the cushion into the glass; in the other it is leaving the glass, and returning into the back part of the cushion. When the prime conductor is apply'd to take it off the glass, the back crescent disappears.

[11] Gilt paper, with the gilt face next the glass, does well.

[12] See farther experiments, § 15.

the air never draws off an electric atmosphere from any body, but in proportion to the non-electrics mix'd with it: it rather keeps such an atmosphere confin'd, which from the mutual repulsion of its particles, tends to dissipation, and would immediately dissipate *in vacuo*.—And thus the experiment of the feather inclosed in a glass vessel hermetically sealed, but moving on the approach of the rubbed tube, is explained: When an additional quantity of the electrical fluid is applied to the side of the vessel by the atmosphere of the tube, a quantity is repelled and driven out of the inner surface of that side into the vessel, and there affects the feather, returning again into its pores, when the tube with its atmosphere is withdrawn; not that the particles of that atmosphere did themselves pass through the glass to the feather.——And every other appearance I have yet seen, in which glass and electricity are concern'd, are, I think, explain'd with equal ease by the same hypothesis. Yet, perhaps, it may not be a true one, and I shall be obliged to him that affords me a better.

35. Thus I take the difference between non electrics and glass, an electric *per se*, to consist in these two particulars. 1st, That a non-electric easily suffers a change in the quantity of the electrical fluid it contains. You may lessen its whole quantity by drawing out a part, which the whole body will again resume; but of glass you can only lessen the quantity contain'd in one of its surfaces; and not that, but by supplying an equal quantity at the same time to the other surface; so that the whole glass may always have the same quantity in the two surfaces, their two different quantities being added together. And this can only be done in glass that is thin; beyond a certain thickness we have yet no power that can make this change. And, 2dly, that the electrical fire freely removes from place to place, in and through the substance of a non-electric, but not so through the substance of glass. If you offer a quantity to one end of a long rod of metal, it receives it, and when it enters, every particle that was before in the rod, pushes its neighbour quite to the further end, where the overplus is discharg'd; and this instantaneously where the rod is part of the circle in the experiment of the shock. But glass, from the smallness of its pores, or stronger attraction of what it contains, refuses to admit so free a motion; a glass rod will not conduct a shock, nor will the thinnest glass suffer any particle entring one of its surfaces to pass thro' to the other.

36. Hence we see the impossibility of success, in the experiments propos'd, to draw out the effluvial virtues of a non-electric, as cinnamon for instance, and mixing them with the electrical fluid, to convey them with that into the body, by including it in the globe, and then applying friction, etc. For though the effluvia of cinnamon, and the electrical fluid should mix within the globe, they would never come out together through the pores of the glass, and so go to the prime conductor; for the electrical fluid itself cannot come through; and the prime conductor is always supply'd from the cushion, and that from the floor. And besides, when the globe is filled with cinnamon, or other non-electric, no electrical fluid can be obtain'd from its outer surface, for the reason before-mentioned. I have try'd another way, which I thought more likely to obtain a mixture of the electrical and other effluvia together, if such a mixture had been possible. I placed a glass plate under my cushion, to cut off the communication between the cushion and floor; then

brought a small chain from the cushion into a glass of oil of turpentine, and carried another chain from the oil of turpentine to the floor, taking care that the chain from the cushion to the glass touch'd no part of the frame of the machine. Another chain was fix'd to the prime conductor, and held in the hand of a person to be electrised. The ends of the two chains in the glass were near an inch distant from each other, the oil of turpentine between. Now the globe being turn'd, could draw no fire from the floor through the machine, the communication that way being cut off by the thick glass plate under the cushion: it must then draw it through the chains whose ends were dipt in the oil of turpentine. And as the oil of turpentine being an electric *per se*, would not conduct what came up from the floor, was obliged to jump from the end of one chain, to the end of the other, through the substance of that oil, which we could see in large sparks; and so it had a fair opportunity of seizing some of the finest particles of the oil in its passage, and carrying them off with it: but no such effect followed, nor could I perceive the least difference in the smell of the electrical effluvia thus collected, from what it has when collected otherwise; nor does it otherwise affect the body of a person electrised. I likewise put into a phial, instead of water, a strong purgative liquid, and then charged the phial, and took repeated shocks from it, in which case every particle of the electrical fluid must, before it went through my body, have first gone through the liquid when the phial is charging, and returned through it when discharging, yet no other effect followed than if it had been charged with water. I have also smelt the electrical fire when drawn through gold, silver, copper, lead, iron, wood, and the human body, and could perceive no difference; the odour is always the same where the spark does not burn what it strikes; and therefore I imagine it does not take that smell from any quality of the bodies it passes through. And indeed, as that smell so readily leaves the electrical matter, and adheres to the knuckle receiving the sparks, and to other things; I suspect that it never was connected with it, but arises instantaneously from something in the air acted upon by it. For if it was fine enough to come with the electrical fluid through the body of one person, why should it stop on the skin of another?

But I shall never have done, if I tell you all my conjectures, thoughts, and imaginations, on the nature and operations of this electrical fluid, and relate the variety of little experiments we have try'd. I have already made this paper too long, for which I must crave pardon, not having now time to make it shorter. I shall only add, that as it has been observed here that spirits will fire by the electrical spark in the summer time, without heating them, when *Fahrenheit*'s thermometer is above 70; so, when colder, if the operator puts a small flat bottle of spirits in his bosom, or a close pocket, with the spoon, some little time before he uses them, the heat of his body will communicate warmth more than sufficient for the purpose.

ADDITIONAL EXPERIMENT, *proving that the* Leyden Bottle *has no more electrical Fire in it when charged, than before; nor less when discharged: That in discharging, the Fire does not issue from the Wire and the Coating at the same Time, as some have thought, but that the Coating always receives what is discharged by the Wire, or an equal Quantity; the outer Surface being always in a negative State of Electric-*

ity, when the inner Surface is in a positive State.

Place a thick plate of glass under the rubbing cushion, to cut off the communication of electrical fire from the floor to the cushion; then, if there be no fine points or hairy threads sticking out from the cushion, or from the parts of the machine opposite to the cushion, (of which you must be careful) you can get but a few sparks from the prime conductor, which are all the cushion will part with.

Hang a phial then on the prime conductor, and it will not charge, tho' you hold it by the coating.— —But

Form a communication by a chain from the coating to the cushion, and the phial will charge.

For the globe then draws the electrical fire out of the outside surface of the phial, and forces it, through the prime conductor and wire of the phial, into the inside surface.

Thus the bottle is charged with its own fire, no other being to be had while the glass plate is under the cushion.

Hang two cork balls by flaxen threads to the prime conductor; then touch the coating of the bottle, and they will be electrified and recede from each other.

For just as much fire as you give the coating, so much is discharged through the wire upon the prime conductor, whence the cork balls receive an electrical atmosphere. But

Take a wire bent in the form of a C, with a stick of wax fixed to the outside of the curve, to hold it by; and apply one end of this wire to the coating, and the other at the same time to the prime conductor, the phial will be discharged; and if the balls are not electrified before the discharge, neither will they appear to be so after the discharge, for they will not repel each other.

Now if the fire discharged from the inside surface of the bottle through its wire, remained on the prime conductor, the balls would be electrified and recede from each other.

If the phial really exploded at both ends, and discharged fire from both coating and wire, the balls would be *more* electrified and recede *farther*: for none of the fire can escape, the wax handle preventing.

But if the fire, with which the inside surface is surcharged, be so much precisely as is wanted by the outside surface, it will pass round through the wire fixed to the wax handle, restore the equilibrium in the glass, and make no alteration in the state of the prime conductor.

Accordingly we find, that if the prime conductor be electrified, and the cork balls in a state of repellency before the bottle is charged, they continue so afterwards. If not, they are not electrified by that discharge.

CORRECTIONS AND ADDITIONS
TO THE PRECEDING PAPERS.

Page 1, Sect. 1. We since find, that the fire in the bottle is not contained in the non-electric, but *in the glass*. All that is after said of the *top* and *bottom* of the bottle, is true of the *inside* and *outside* surfaces, and should have been so expressed. *See Sect.* 16, p. 16.

Page 3, Line 13. The equilibrium will soon be restored *but silently*, etc. This must have been a mistake. When the bottle is full charged, the crooked wire cannot well be brought to touch the top and bottom so quick, but that there will be a loud spark; unless the points be sharp, without loops.

Ibid. line ult. *Outside*: add, such moisture continuing up to the cork or wire.

Page 7, line 14. *By candle-light* etc. From some observations since made, I am inclined to think, that it is not the light, but the smoke or non-electric effluvia from the candle, coal, and red-hot iron, that carry off the electrical fire, being first attracted and then repelled.

Page 7, line 15. *Windmil wheels*, &c. We afterwards discovered, that the afflux or efflux of the electrical fire, was not the cause of the motions of those wheels, but various circumstances of attraction and repulsion.

Page 9, line 21. *Let* A *and* B *stand on wax*, &c. We soon found that it was only necessary for one of them to stand on wax.

Page 11. in the title r. *on*.

Page 13, line 12. r. contact, line 24. confined.

Page 14, line 10. for *stand* r. *hand*.

Page 15, line 2. *The consequence might perhaps be fatal*, &c. We have found it fatal to small animals, but 'tis not strong enough to kill large ones. The biggest we have killed is a hen.

Page 16, line 20. *Ringing of chimes*, &c. This is since done.

Page 17, line 22. *Fails after ten or twelve experiments*. This was by a small bottle. And since found to fail after with a large glass.

Page 24, sect. 50, 51. *Spirits must be heated before we can fire them*, &c. We have since fired spirits without heating, when the weather is warm.

FINIS.

Lector House believes that a society develops through a two-fold approach of continuous learning and adaptation, which is derived from the study of classic literary works spread across the historic timeline of literature records. Therefore, we aim at reviving, repairing and redeveloping all those inaccessible or damaged but historically as well as culturally important literature across subjects so that the future generations may have an opportunity to study and learn from past works to embark upon a journey of creating a better future.

This book is a result of an effort made by Lector House towards making a contribution to the preservation and repair of original ancient works which might hold historical significance to the approach of continuous learning across subjects.

HAPPY READING & LEARNING!

LECTOR HOUSE LLP
E-MAIL: lectorpublishing@gmail.com